CHINESE MUSIC
FOR GUITAR

BY FERNANDO PÉREZ

T0081339

ISBN 978-1-4950-1158-0

HAL•LEONARD®
7777 W. BLUEMOUND RD. P.O. BOX 13819 MILWAUKEE, WI 53213

In Australia Contact:
Hal Leonard Australia Pty. Ltd.
4 Lentara Court
Cheltenham, 3192 Victoria, Australia
Email: ausadmin@halleonard.com.au

Visit Hal Leonard Online at
www.halleonard.com

CONTENTS

INTRODUCTION

Since I was very young I have dedicated my life to studying music and how to play guitar in different styles. As I grew older and progressed through the common styles available on the instrument, I found in my love for different cultures a new ground to discover other styles which would lend themselves to be played on the guitar.

I enjoy performing Middle Eastern music on fretless guitar or West African music on nylon or steel strings. But what really makes me feel fulfilled is to be able to find new ways of playing my favorite instrument while helping to keep alive ancient traditions; these traditions carry not only music but wisdom.

In many cases we could say these traditions are endangered. I have been a witness of this fact through personal experience; in every place I move to in order to learn directly from the culture, I find a big percentage of youngsters more interested in modern mainstream commercial styles than their own traditional music. For these and many other reasons I feel fortunate enough to do something I love in life, and at the same time contribute to a major cause.

Studying Chinese music is like finding a huge mine full of a variety of precious stones barely touched. This musical tradition offers a turning point in guitar playing. The character and variety of music compositions, the styles found in instruments like Pipa or Guqin which lend themselves so well to the guitar, bring such a scope of new techniques, textures and sounds for the instrument. And most important is the approach to performing the music, teaching us how to tap into artistic depths never imagined. If we add to these the high human values embodied in this music, we obtain a recipe for becoming a master musician and a better human being.

Fernando Pérez

Shanghai, China 2012

ABOUT CHINESE TRADITIONAL MUSIC

China has always been a vast land rich in cultural movements. The large variety of ethnic groups with their traditions have shaped Chinese music in a very interesting way. This has evolved together with culture, absorbing customs from no fewer than about fifty ethnic groups, each one having its own traditional music. The majority is constituted by the Han people. This is why although Chinese music should include music of all its people, in reality we generally refer to Han music, often not including music of groups considered as "minorities."

But to truly understand, experience, and be able to play Chinese music regardless of what specific style-tradition we choose, we need to know its people and the way they look at music and life. This is important especially if the student has been raised in the West and has never been exposed to the way the ancient Chinese used to think and value life.

Chinese people have always been very attached to nature and its laws. We can find a trace of this all over, from martial arts movements derived from watching animals' behavior, to paintings that try to bring alive the magnificent beauty of landscapes and nature sites. Music happens exactly the same; we often come across tunes with names such as "White Snow in the Spring Sunlight" or the popular "Flowing Water." All of them depict with sound the wonders of nature.

In Chinese writings which are referred to as a source for wisdom, we find many passages talking about music. Among them we have the *Analects*, *Liji*, and many others. One of the most influential masters of wisdom for Chinese people (and even nowadays for Westerners) is Lao Tse and his *Tao Te Ching*. In it the sage explains how we ought to learn from nature and respect its flow. Lao Tse's teachings awoke a new sense of consciousness always related to nature and applied to every single action in life, including music.

But if we want straightforward direction on how to approach Chinese music and its relation to people, we just need to follow the ancient but still latent teachings of Confucius. In the *Analects* (Confucius' sayings) we find him saying, "Arouse through poetry, balance yourself with ritualized action and make yourself complete with music." For this master the art that completes people's character is music. In Confucianism the importance of music lies in its harmonizing power, believing that if music balances the individual's character, it can also harmonize and balance society. For this reason it was said that "music is the harmony of Heaven and Earth." Confucius added that music that is noble and spiritual in nature draws men into inner centered peaceful absortion, opening the heart to deep transformative spiritual energies, thus completing a person's character.

The *Liji* or "Book of Rituals" is a collection of writings by Confucius's students. One of its chapters is called *Yueji* ("Music Statement") and is one of the only surviving ancient Chinese writings dealing with music and ritual. Its overall vision is that of the world being transformed through music. One of its main ideas is, "If a person is not sensitive to others' suffering, of what use is music?" A person since young years is attracted to harmonious sounds, and this sensitivity can be developed through the following years of his/her life, thus developing compassion towards others. If it does not happen this way the person will lack the sensitivity neccesary to relate to others with compassion and kindness.

The meaning and function of the arts thus extends far beyond individual self-cultivation, as a means for creating self-aware, self-confident, and educated individuals who can lead and instruct society without being easily manipulated. This applies not only to Chinese, but to all people around the globe.

In the *Liji* it was also realized that rituals are important, because men learn how to let go of the self and reharmonize with cosmic powers as well as making any social clashes disappear. Dance was, and still is, a collective ritualization of movement. This is extended to the player, for it is not only the dancer but also the player who sways to sound and rhythm. Music creates a flow of *Qi* or vital energy emanating from the player and spreading outwards to those present in the musical "ceremony" of a live performance. Hence if one wants to really appreciate and enjoy the depths of Chinese traditional music; like in any other style of music; the best option is always to attend a live performance where the real Qi (or in this case "musical energy") flows freely for those who really want to experience life in the most pure state.

But this musical philosophy did not originally come from Confucius. The master himself was actually captivated by the astonishing effects of what is called *Shao* music.

Shao music was and has been one of the highest revered genres for its elegance and completeness, including a perfect combination of poetry, music and dance. It is also considered the best of ancient Chinese court music. Its impact on people has been so deep that we even find legends referring to it. An example is how Emperor Shundi was besieged by the Miao tribesmen who dropped their weapons and started dancing to the sound of Shundi's men playing Shao music.

From this humble writer's point of view, through all these explanations one can understand that this way of performing music is worth preserving and bringing back into our modern times. It is a treasure to society and spiritual life and its value goes far beyond the level of treating music as simple entertainment.

THE CHINESE TRADITIONAL MUSIC SYSTEM

History and Meaning

Chinese music has developed its tuning and notation systems over three thousand years without being influenced by the western world. It only received a small influence from neighboring areas such as India (through Buddhist practices), Korea, and Persia. But in the second half of the nineteenth century, western music started making impact in China. Group singing and instrumental playing practices were not in use in traditional Chinese music until that time. In the early twentieth century, western music and its theory highly attracted Chinese composers, inspiring them even to travel abroad in order to study it and later apply it to their own traditions.

Nevertheless, we have to bear in mind that Chinese traditional music is mostly monophonic; there is no harmony. At times the counterpoint of certain base tones with melody notes might produce a harmony or chord effect to the ear, but is never treated in the western way.

Just as we find in other Eastern music traditions, like the Classical music of India, Chinese music has a very personal approach when it comes to learning musical notes. Every sound is considered as a being with identity, character, and a way of behaving or reacting when interacting with another. For instance, Chinese Confucianists developed a way to correlate the five primary notes of the music scale with the structure of a government.

- The *Gōng* note, being the deepest and giving a kind of base with its sonority, represented the ruler.

- The *Shāng* note, lighter because of its position in the scale, represented the ministers.

- The *Jué* note, one step after *Shāng*, represented the people.

- The *Zhí* note represented the affairs.

- The *Yǔ* note was the lightest and represented the material resources which gave shape to the way of implementing the government of all.

Hence we can understand how disorder in any of the different levels would produce disorder in the rest, and absence of disorder between them would produce harmony in the government as well as the music. If the *Gōng* note is unbalanced the music will become lost, like a nation with a king excessively proud. If the *Shāng* note is out of balance the music will become off-center, as if ministers were delinquent in their duties. If the *Jué* note is unbalanced, music can become sorrowful, meaning people will have many reasons to complain to their government. If the *Zhí* note is out of balance, music will sound full of sadness, maybe for the excess of work imposed on people to keep up with their lifestyle. And if the *Yǔ* note is unbalanced, music will take a dangerous quality, as if people have become extremely poor. If all five notes are out of balance, each one trying to be more than the others, the total lack of respect for each other will produce a collapse of the whole.

This is a very interesting way of looking at music and reflecting what is going on around us. We can notice this in the kind of music made by people who might be complaining about something. Likewise we can discern them from people feeling perfect balance in their lives, just by observing the balance in their musical notes. The best and easiest example would be to look at our current society and the many music styles created through the years. Where do they come from? Were they a result of something happening in society? How are the people who play them or feel attracted to them? What feelings do these styles produce in us as we listen to them? Ancient Chinese sages knew and could foretell so many things about people, their spirits, society, and development of events just by observing or practicing the art of music.

Notation Systems

It is very important to forget the western way of thinking about notes mathematically, with a determined height giving a pitch which might be organized in certain ways established by music theory. The key is to treat notes as sounds which are alive and with personalities of their own. Needless to say, the Chinese music system uses a blend of tempered and untempered notes. These two are used in such fluency that the best way to learn is by oral tradition and listening rather than over-analyzing.

In traditional Chinese music, the method of writing music has always been challenging. This is due to the use of different styles of music notation like *Gongche*, *Jianpu*, etc., in different periods of history. All of these styles were based in a tablature type of writing. Nowadays the western music notation system is also used, but the fact is that writing music in China was always a way of sketching the basic idea of the tune. The real way of learning how to perform music has always come and still comes from the direct instruction of a music master. Even in this book it is highly recommended to follow the score as a guide and really pay close attention to the video. Listening well to the intention of every note or musical phrase is key to performing them correctly.

In Chinese music, like in all music traditions around the World, the music notes come from the harmonic series. In our case, the harmonics were produced in bamboo pipes, bells, or even stringed instruments like the *Guqin*. This is what we call a *natural* or *untempered* system of pitches. The pitches coming out of this are called *Lü*. Far from being a scale, they are just the notes available to build scales or modes on. As time went by and Chinese musicians were exposed to western music, the pitches started to get mixed with tempered sounds. Today we can hear, depending on the instrument placed, music that is more tempered-sounding.

In our case with the Spanish guitar, when imitating the *Pipa* style of playing, most notes are tempered. There are exceptions made, however, when we play notes by way of bending strings or using natural harmonics and glissandos. In the case of the *Guqin* style performed on a fretless guitar, we have fewer technical limitations so we can play more accurately natural untempered pitches.

From all the pitches Chinese musicians produced, five main sounds or notes have been established and are used nowadays. Their names, as mentioned above, are: *Gōng*, *Shāng*, *Jué*, *Zhí*, and *Yǔ*. If we were to put them in western notes they would have this interval relationship:

Example 1

You have probably already realized how these notes make a major pentatonic scale with degrees 1, 2, 3, 5, 6. *Gōng* (1) is the first note, *Shāng* (2) one step up, *Jué* (3) another step up, *Zhí* (5) one step and a half up, and finally *Yǔ* (6) one step up. *Gōng*, a step and a half higher, completes the octave.

This relationship of notes can be used starting from different notes, giving us different keys.

Major Pentatonic Scale from D

Example 2

Major Pentatonic Scale from G

Example 3

In the last two examples the interval relationship of the notes is the same. We also use the same Chinese names for the notes. This is known in western European music as the "movable C" system. Every time we have this note relationship, even if it starts from a different root (first note), the notes will have the same name.

Now if we take this scale and preserve the interval relationship between its pitches, starting from different notes we will obtain four other different scales or modes. This will give us a total of five available modes. If you have studied the Greek modes in western music, you will find a similar approach in obtaining the Chinese modes or scales. But be aware, because although the contruction is similar the use will be different. These five Chinese modes will be named after their starting notes.

Gōng Mode

Example 4

Shāng Mode

Example 5

Jué Mode

Example 6

Zhí Mode

Example 7

Yǔ Mode

Example 8

These modes could be played in different keys. All we need to do is to keep the same interval relationship between the notes of the mode we want to play.

Jué Mode in G

Example 9

Zhí Mode in F

Example 10

Playing these modes on the guitar, you will realize they are the same five modes of the pentatonic scale so commonly used in guitar styles. The wonderful thing about Chinese music is that you will be playing these familiar scales but they will sound quite different than usual.

Gōng Modes (Major Pentatonic Scale)

Example 11

Shāng Mode

Example 12

Jué Mode

Example 13

Zhí Mode

Example 14

Yǔ Mode (Minor Pentatonic Scale)

Example 15

Sometimes a scale note can be played a half step down. This note then becomes an altered version of the original, called in Chinese a *Biàn* note.

Biàn notes are used as grace notes or to help modulate from one mode to another. To know what specific note has been altered, we put Biàn together with the name of the original note, like *Biànzhí* (biàn + zhí) or *Biángōng* (biàn + gōng).

11

PIPA STYLE GUITAR TECHNIQUES

Fernando Pérez holding a Pipa.
Shangai Music Conservatory, China.

In China we find some of the oldest musical instruments still in use today. In this land where the earliest instruments can be traced as far back as 6000–5000 years B.C., it is no surprise to find such peculiar ones as the *Pipa* or *Guqin*.

The Pipa is a stringed instrument very close to the guitar. In a way it's part of its family of ancestors by way of a connected line between the Indian *Sarod*, the Arabic *Oud*, and others. It typically has four strings, a fretboard similar to the guitar, and even playing techniques that are similar to the guitar.

It is thanks to this old instrument that we find in our modern times new techniques which can be applied to the guitar. The first thing we need to do in order to get closer to this instrument's playing techniques and sound is to adjust our guitar tuning using the following notes from sixth to first string: E–A–D–E–A–E.

You probably noticed that we have changed only two strings: the third down to E and second to A. Getting used to this tuning is very easy.

Tremolo

One of the techniques most used for playing melodies is tremolo. On the guitar we find many different types of tremolos. We can use a classical tremolo which is performed by using the right hand thumb (p), ring (a), middle (m), and index (i) fingers in this specific order. This example uses standard guitar tuning.

Example 16

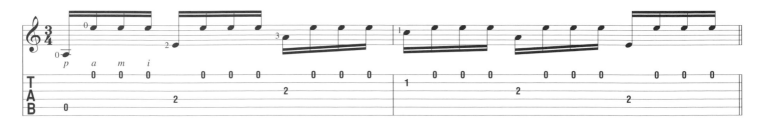

In this example we can notice the finger order and also the function of this specific technique. In many classical tremolo styles, the thumb plays an arpeggiated chord while the rest of the fingers play the actual tremolo on one note. In other cases the thumb plays a specific melody. At times the melody is played in the tremolo notes by ring, middle, and index fingers, while the thumb keeps a bass note or arpeggio.

The same thing happens in flamenco-style tremolo. This has very similar functions as the classical, but the tremolo notes become busier since we use an extra finger strike. The finger order in the right hand would be: thumb, index, ring, middle, index. Here is the last example in a flamenco version. (The example is in standard tuning.)

Example 17

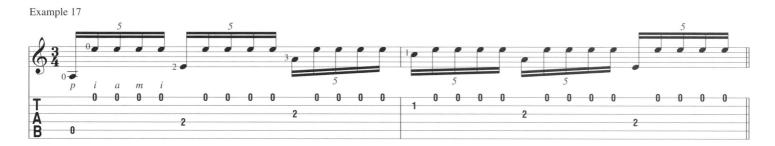

These two types of tremolo are not restricted to their original styles. Personally I have used both in many other styles. As a matter of fact, functions aside, I use one or the other in relation to the tempo of the piece. For instance, busier flamenco-style tremolos sound too stressful in fast tempos, whereas classical ones flow really well.

In Chinese music we find the Pipa—and now the guitar—using thumb, little (c), ring, middle, and index fingers. At first sight this seems like the other tremolos we just spoke of, but if we take a look at the functions we see how different they really are. In the other two tremolos the thumb's function was separated from the rest of the fingers; in Chinese music it is not. The five fingers create a complete tremolo effect dedicated to playing melodies.

In this book there are many notes played by tremolo, so instead of writing every note as is usually done, the "three lines" tremolo sign is used. In the next example, the first measure shows the notes written with the tremolo sign, and the second shows how they are actually played.

Example 18

Take a look now at a few measures from the tune "Heroic Little Sisters" to see how a melody with tremolo is written. The following examples are in Chinese Pipa guitar tuning (E–A–D–E–A–E).

Example 19
Tuning (low to high): E-A-D-E-A-E

But playing just the melody is not the only function of Chinese tremolo. It can also work as in the classical and flamenco styles, playing melody and bass notes.

Here are a few measures from "Heroic Little Sisters" using the same type of tremolo, but every time we have a bass note this is played by the thumb. Watch the video for a deeper look at what is happening with the right hand.

Example 20
Tuning (low to high): E-A-D-E-A-E

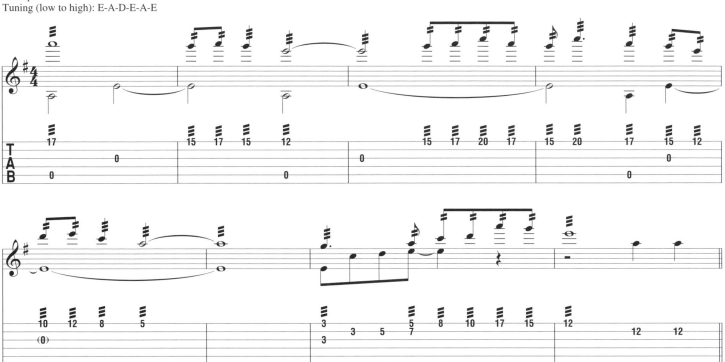

In the next example you will see something quite common, combining everything. You will notice in the third measure a quasi-tremolo followed by a full tremolo in the next measure. All tremolos here are combined with normally-plucked notes.

Example 21
Tuning (low to high): E-A-D-E-A-E

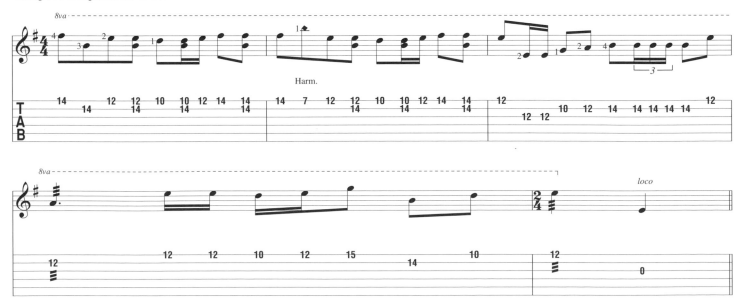

It is important to note that Chinese players—in this case Pipa players—seem to use their fingers in an "upside-down" way. For instance, the tremolo in the last example uses the finger order thumb–little–ring–middle–index, whereas a Chinese player would use thumb–index–middle–ring–little. For guitarists the most familiar way would be the first, but do not make the mistake of distinguishing between "right" and "wrong." In reality both ways are right. As a matter of fact, each way brings a different sound, texture, musical color, or even pulse. For now we can use the familiar guitarist way without sacrificing much of the sound, but later on we will find other techniques dealing with the same situation and it is highly recommended that you follow the Chinese way since it brings the original sound.

The last tremolo we are going to use is played with one finger. This can be executed by your middle finger as well as your index or even ring finger. But remember, only one finger.

The technique is very simple; all you have to do is quickly move your finger playing the string, hitting it upward as well as downward. To differentiate this tremolo from the previous one, it will be notated with the same sign but with only two lines instead of three.

Take a look at another few measures from "Heroic Little Sisters." Again, it is important for you to check out the video explanations of the tune to clear any doubt about what words might fall short of explaining.

Example 22
Tuning (low to high): E-A-D-E-A-E

Contrary "Pi" Picking

Another very curious technique found in Pipa playing is the use of thumb and index finger for picking. In guitar playing, every time we play two notes using these two fingers, the thumb strikes the string downward while the index plucks upwards, and it continues like this in a repeated way. Pipa playing uses this move but also the opposite; the thumb strikes the string going upward while the index does the same moving downward. This is the first move chosen, followed by the "normal" one we know.

Personally, instead of using thumb and index fingers for this way of playing, I use thumb and middle. This frees my index finger in case I need to play artificial harmonics. I highly recommend this, since it offers you broader possibilities—but you can also do it in the original Pipa style using thumb and index.

The notes in this next exercise are played alternating these two movements. Make sure the volume of your notes is even.

Example 23
Tuning (low to high): E-A-D-E-A-E

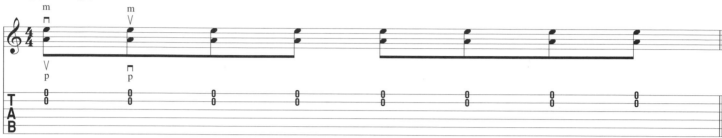

Now try the same thing with a "normal" guitar playing technique. Notice how the sound and especially the pulse of the music sounds different. The "pumping" of the notes changes as we use one or the other option.

Example 24
Tuning (low to high): E-A-D-E-A-E

Here is the technique applied in a passage from the tune "Heroic Little Sisters." You can play it in guitar or Pipa style, but the most authentic sound will eventually come from the Chinese way.

Example 25
Tuning (low to high): E-A-D-E-A-E

Playing Beyond the Fretboard

One of the amazing features of the Pipa is its broad range. It does not reach very low, but it surely goes very high in its upper register. This is quite challenging in the guitar since our upper register does not reach so high. Fortunately we have different techniques available to reach out, or I should say to "reach up."

First and most common is the use of harmonics. We have natural as well as artificial harmonics that we can use in order to play in higher registers. But there is another way to play high notes getting a different tone: playing beyond the fretboard. This means playing notes with the left hand positioned beyond the twentieth fret and up.

It is a relatively simple technique. The first thing we need to do is free our left-hand thumb from behind the guitar's neck. We should have it on the same side as the rest of our fingers over the fretboard. This will liberate our hand from being anchored to the neck. Anchoring is very useful for stability of the left hand, so now that the thumb is not there we will feel a little unsecure. But with a little practice we should be able to overcome this. Now the rest of the fingers will be free to reach over the twentieth fret and further. But you will say, *there are no frets anymore!* And even if you press on the string the sound will be muffled due to the lack of the metal fret. What we will do now is to roll the tip of our finger a little so we are also pressing the string with the nail. The sound will now be brighter and more usable.

Since the nail is not that hard and the string at this point has been shortened quite a lot, our sound will lack sustain. We will end up doing what all kinds of short-sustaining instruments always do: playing tremolo in order to maintain the sound. With any of the tremolo techniques explained previously, along with this way of "fretting beyond frets," we have just broadened our guitar range.

Try this new technique in the intro of "Heroic Little Sisters." The notes in parentheses are to be played off-fretboard.

Example 26
Tuning (low to high): E-A-D-E-A-E

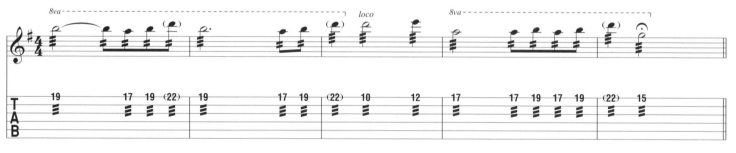

PIPA STYLE MUSIC
for Standard Guitar

The following compositions are based on the Pipa style. The guitar tuning we are using is (from sixth to first string): E–A–D–E–A–E.

MOONLIGHT OVER THE RIVER IN SPRING

This beautiful piece can be found under different names, but the one we are using here is the most common. It comes from a poem of the Tang dynasty speaking about the wonders of nature. In a poetic manner it describes how the moon rises over a river that has overflowed due to the melting snow of spring. Please, do not suffer from the shortcoming of these words to describe the beauty of nature and this poem; both deserve to be observed and enjoyed in depth. It would be better to read the poem or even more, experience what it refers to. Once you have studied this piece, those things will really help you to bring the spirit into the music.

Returning to earthly matters, the composition is divided into three parts, each given a name in order to help you visualize the musical description we are playing.

Make sure you do not rush it. Listen to the recording many times until you can hum or whistle the melody. If you are not a person raised around Chinese culture, it will be challenging to lay yourself back enough to tap into the real pulse of this type of music that is so difficult to write down. Lean more towards listening to the recording than just sticking to the written score. Every important detail will also be explained in the video.

MOONLIGHT OVER THE RIVER IN SPRING

Part 1

Traditional Chinese
Guitar arrangement by Fernando Pérez

Tuning (low to high): E-A-D-E-A-E

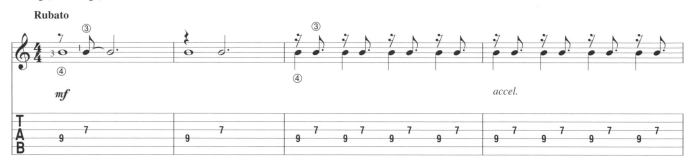

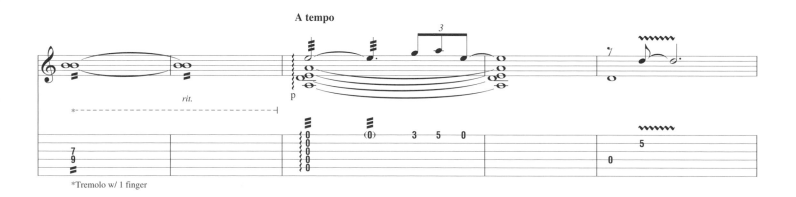

*Tremolo w/ 1 finger

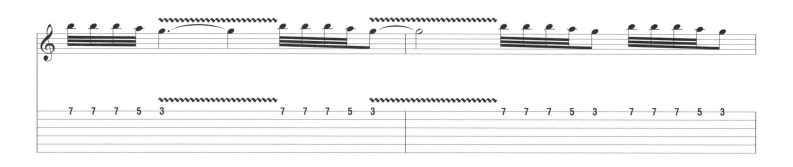

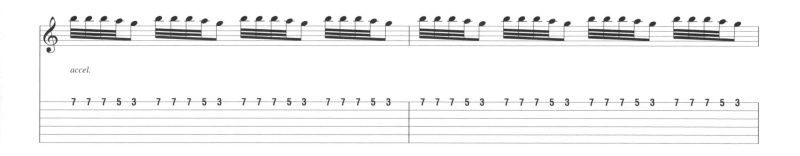

*Pertains to 3rd-5th strings.

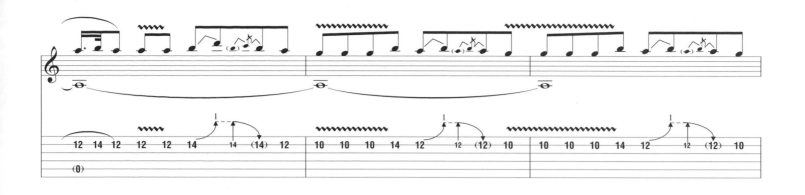

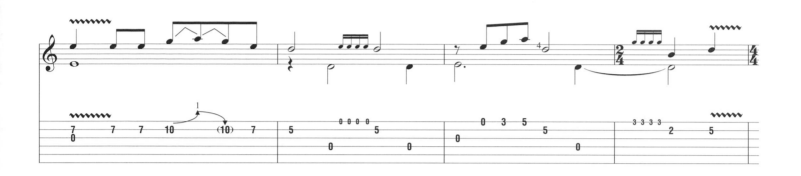

**Touch string near lower ring of rosette w/pick hand thumbnail
while plucking string w/pick hand ring finger.

*As before

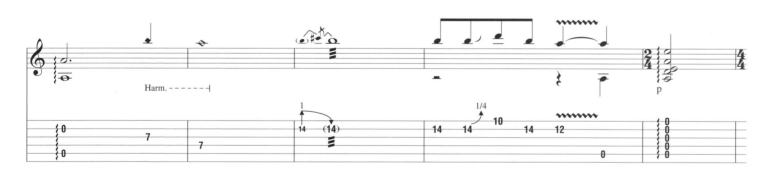

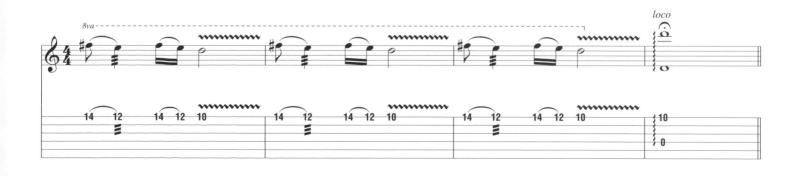

MOONLIGHT OVER THE RIVER IN SPRING

Part 2: Concealing Clouds

Tuning (low to high): E-A-D-E-A-E

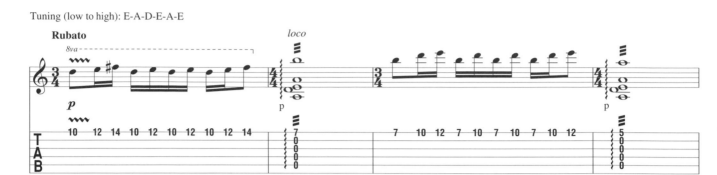

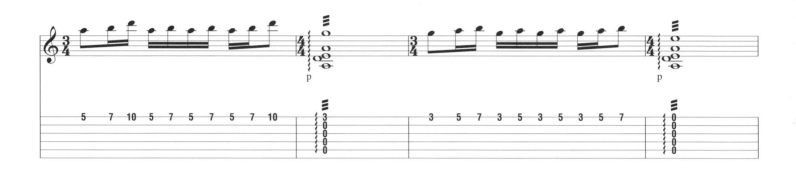

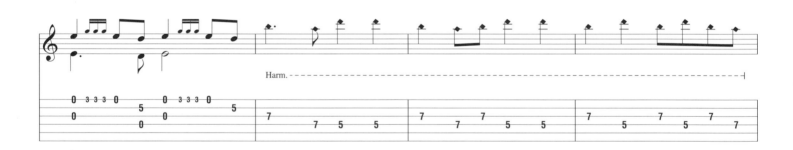

*Artificial Harm.: Lightly touch string at fret number in parentheses w/ picking hand index finger while simultaneously picking fretted note w/ thumb.

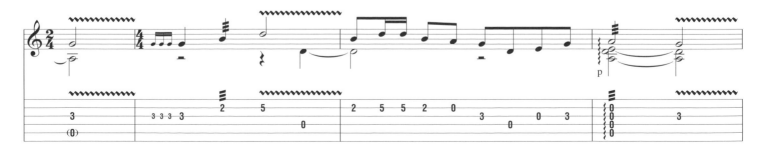

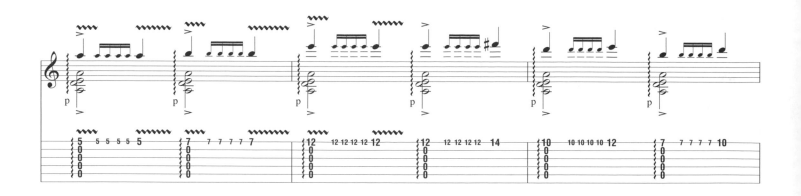

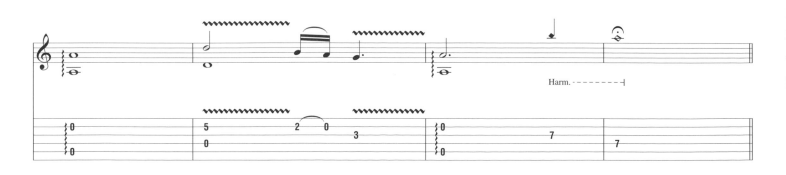

MOONLIGHT OVER THE RIVER IN SPRING

Part 3: Blooming Flowers

Tuning (low to high): E-A-D-E-A-E

*Harm.

*Pertains to 2nd-5th strings throughout.

HEROIC LITTLE SISTERS IN THE GRASSLANDS

This was one of my favorite pieces when I recorded the CD *Traditional Chinese Music for Guitar*, and also the most challenging. But I have to say it was the piece I learned more with. It tells the epic story of two Mongolian girls, Long Mei and Yu Rong, walking in the fields, caring for their herd, facing a terrible storm and marching throughout the freezing night to end up blossoming in a new day. The composition is credited to a collaboration between Pipa master Liu Dehai and composers Wu Zhuqiang and Wang Yanjiao. It is said that most of its melodies were drawn from folk tunes.

Again, the piece has been divided into three parts in order to better understand it and picture every part of the story. We are using the Pipa style guitar tuning E–A–D–E–A–E.

HEROIC LITTLE SISTERS IN THE GRASSLANDS

Part 1

Written by Liu Dehai, Wu Zhuqiang and Wang Yanjiao
(From traditional Chinese folk tunes)
Guitar arrangement by Fernando Pérez

Tuning (low to high): E-A-D-E-A-E

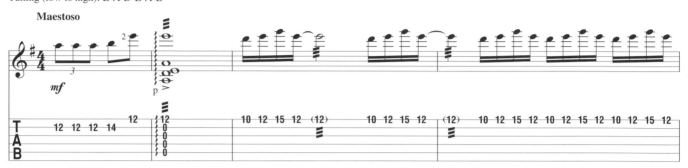

*Hypothetical fret location.
Use fret hand and fingernail.

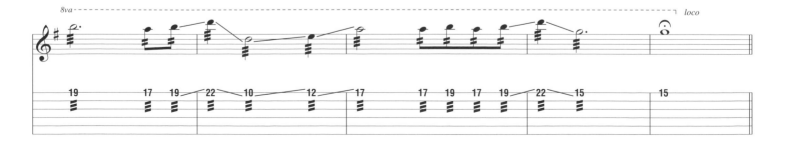

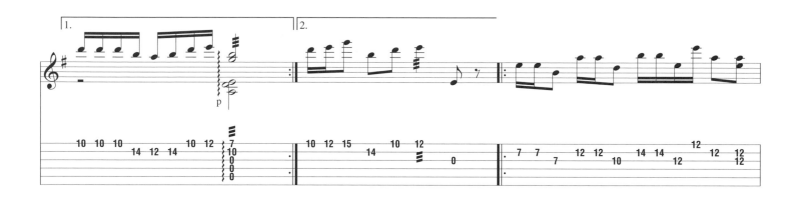

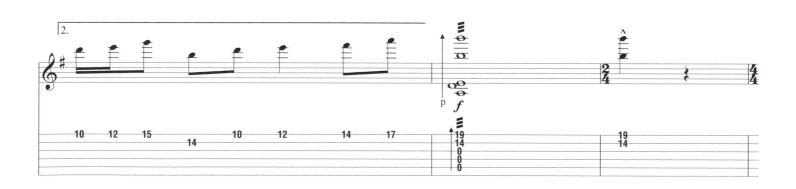

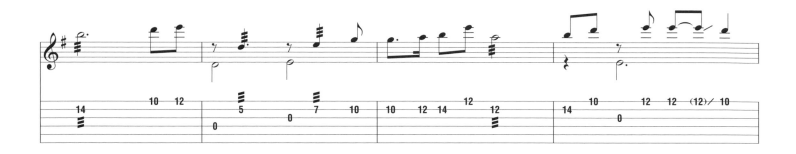

*Hypothetical fret location

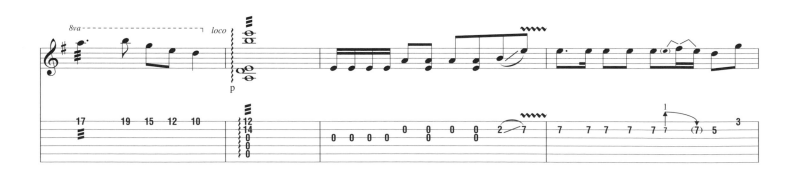

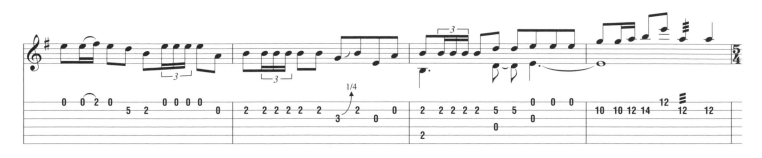

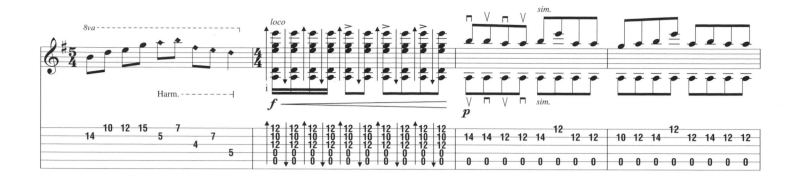

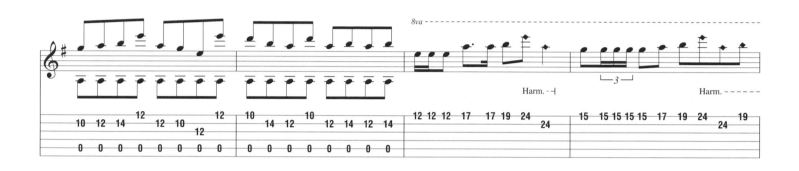

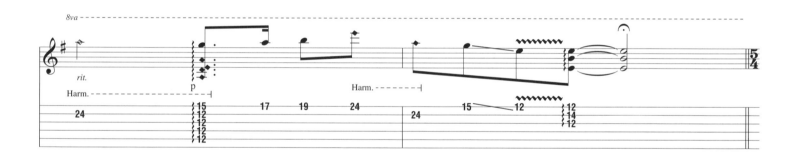

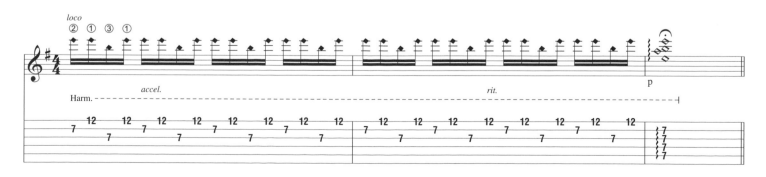

HEROIC LITTLE SISTERS IN THE GRASSLANDS

Part 2: The Storm

Tuning (low to high): E-A-D-E-A-E

Lento

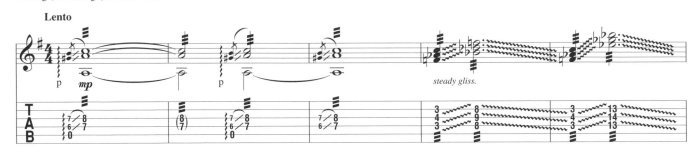

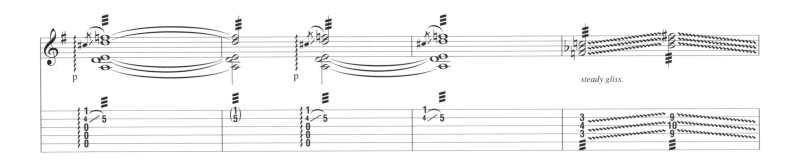

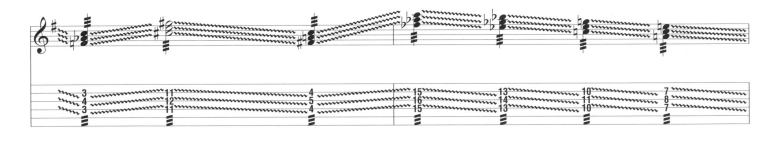

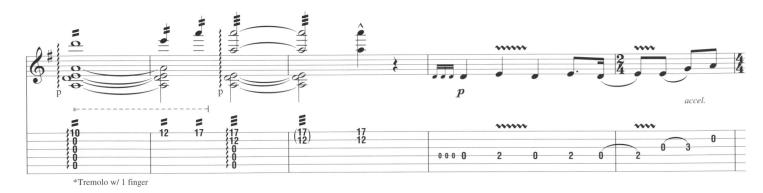

*Tremolo w/ 1 finger

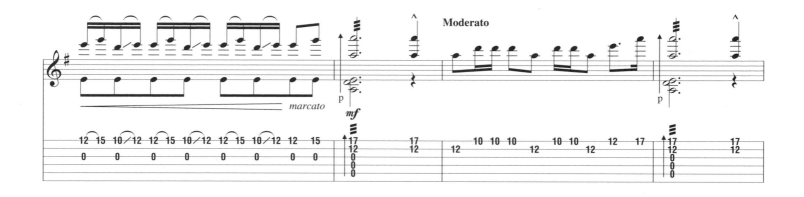

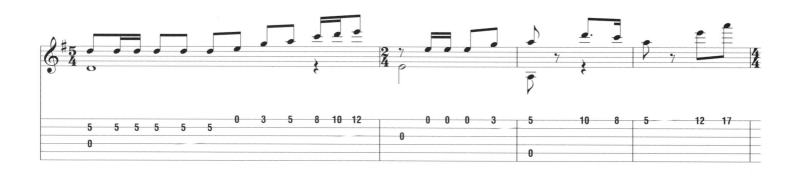

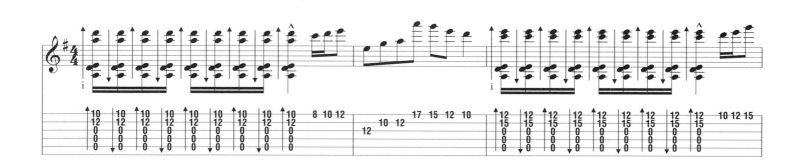

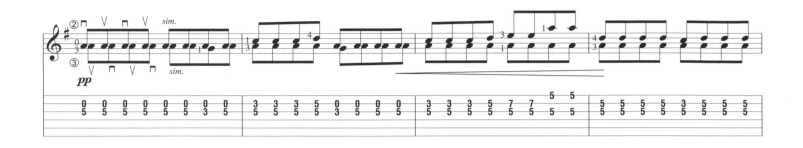

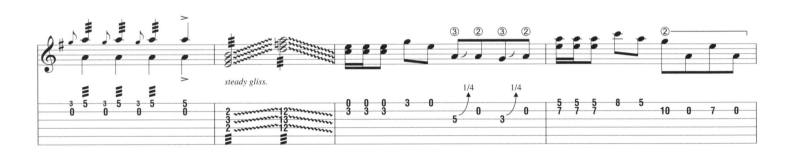

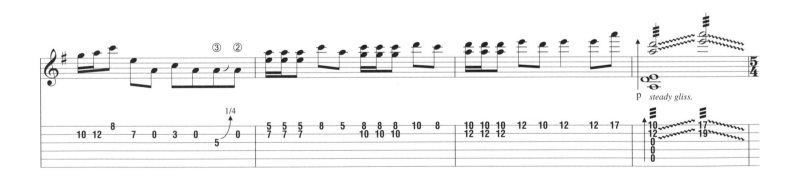

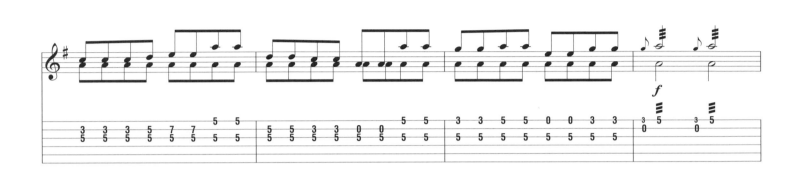

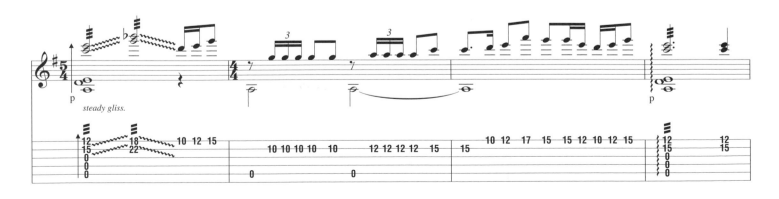

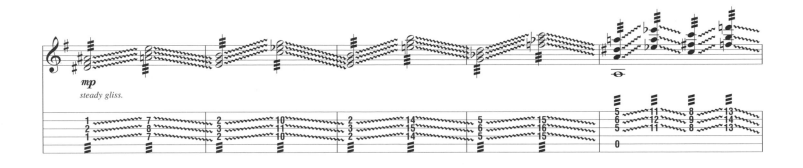

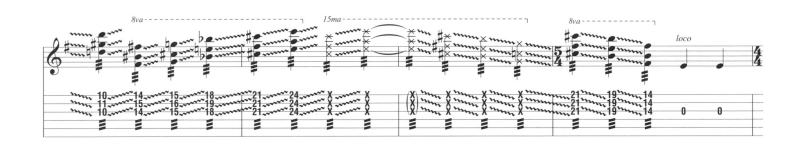

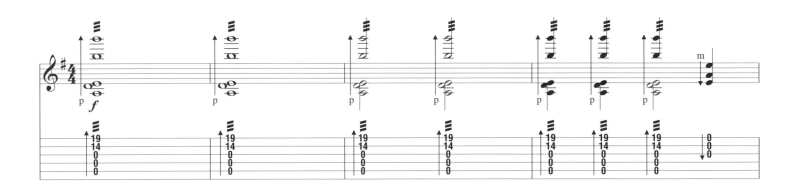

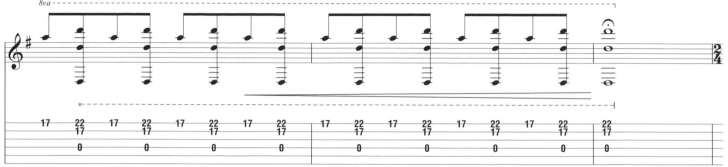

*Fret 2nd string w/ thumb.

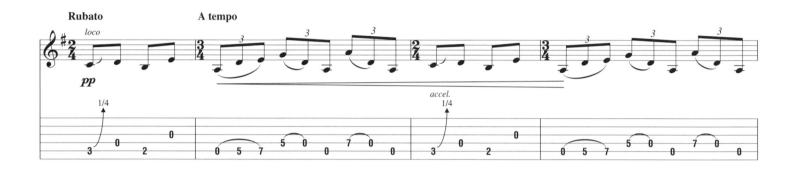

**next 7 meas.

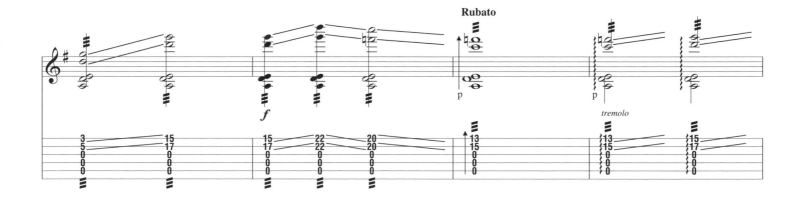

Rubato

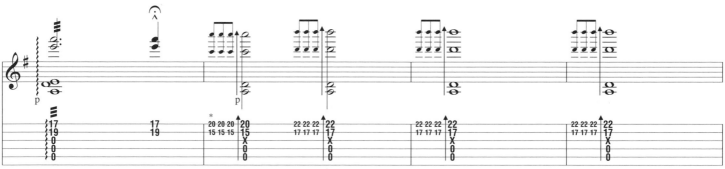

*Fret 2nd string w/ thumb & mute 3rd string w/ index finger of picking hand.

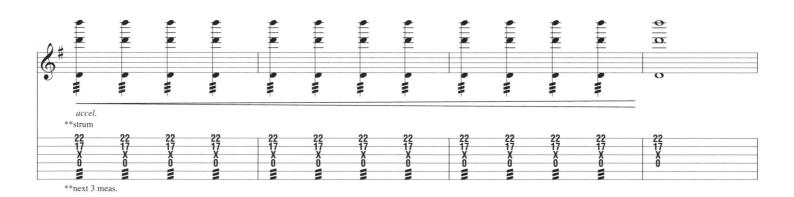

accel.
**strum

**next 3 meas.

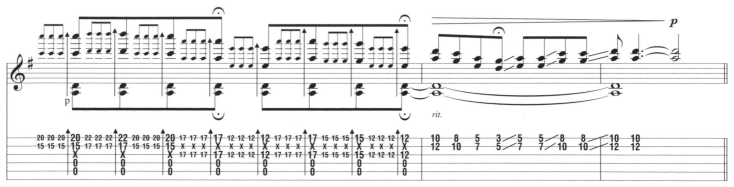

HEROIC LITTLE SISTERS IN THE GRASSLANDS

Part 3: A Brand New Day

Tuning (low to high): E-A-D-E-A-E

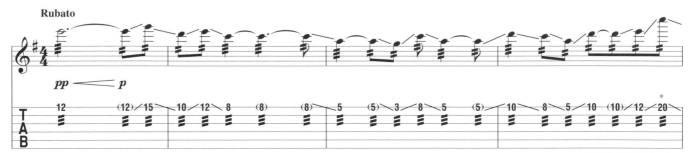

*Hypothetical fret location

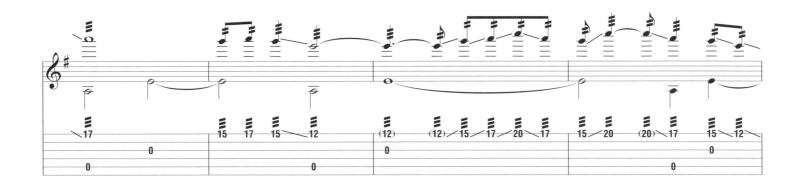

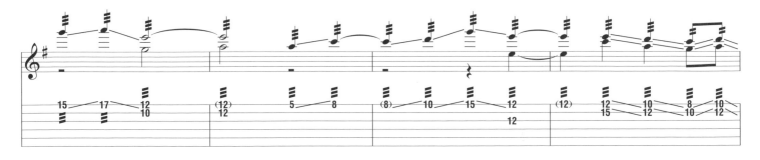

*Tremolo 1st string notes only.

dolce e quasi rubato

**Tremolo w/ 1 finger, next 13 meas.

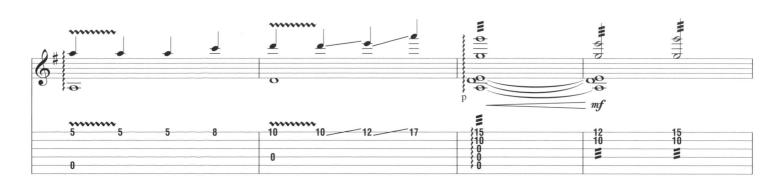

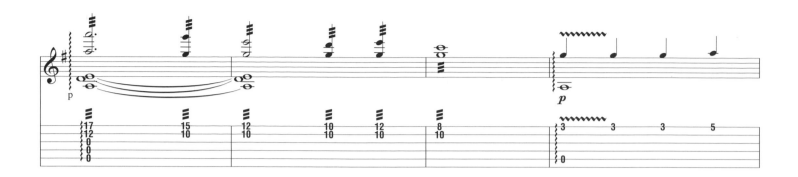

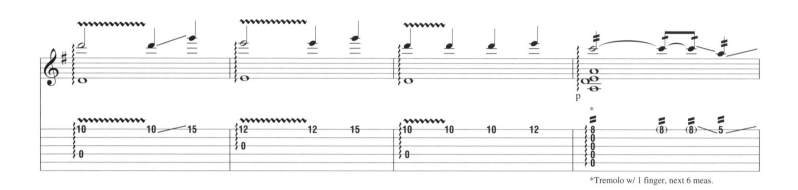

*Tremolo w/ 1 finger, next 6 meas.

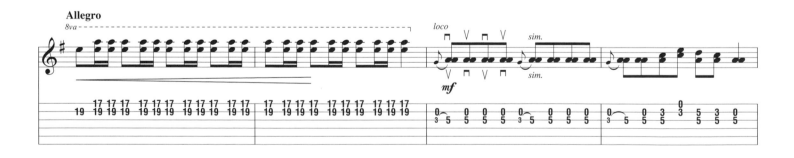

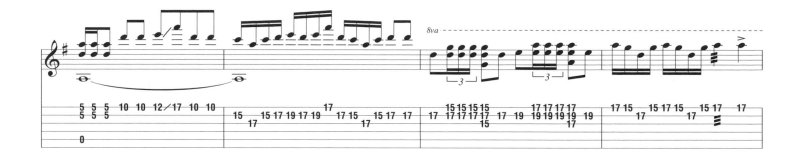

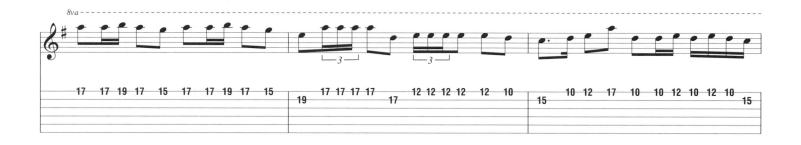

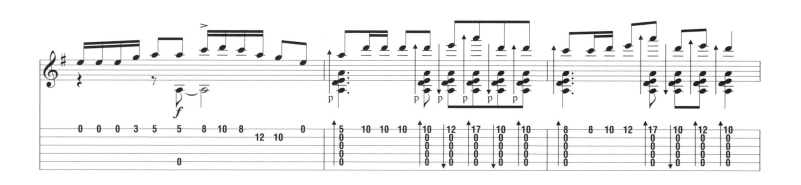

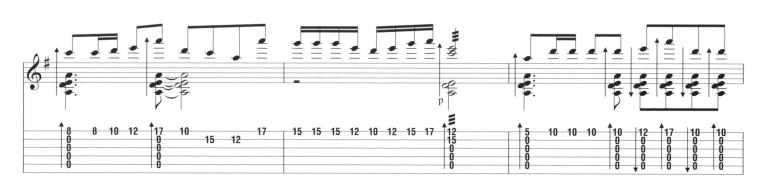

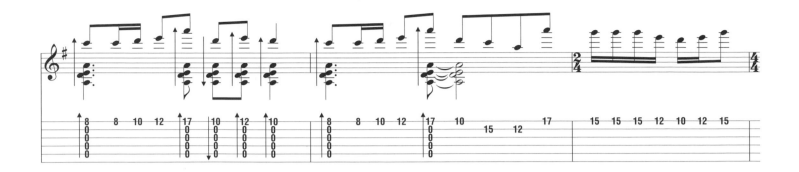

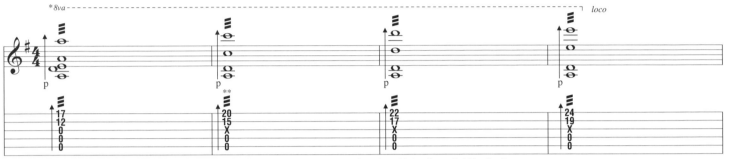

*Applies to top two notes only. **Fret 2nd string w/ thumb and mute 3rd string w/ index finger of picking hand.

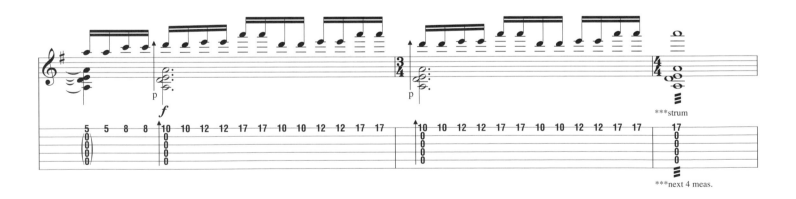

***strum

***next 4 meas.

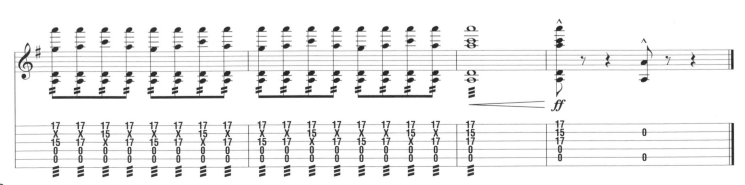

GUQIN STYLE GUITAR TECHNIQUES

The *Guqin* is one of the oldest instruments still in use today. In ancient China it was always related to high education and culture standards. Among the several tasks a learned person should undertake, one was learning to play Guqin, or *Qin* as it is usually referred to.

The instrument itself is a seven-stringed zither, but not any kind of zither. Almost every part constituting this instrument has a very deep meaning, relating to elements which tap into the human spirit. For instance, the original Guqins had five strings, symbolizing the five elements. Two more strings were added later, also related to different feelings and situations. Even the inlays are related to the months of the lunar calendar.

One can really understand to what extent this instrument reaches the soul just by listening to its sound. For some westerners, tapping into these musical depths can be a little challenging at the beginning. It is quite a personal exercise to tune in to the instrument's sound, but once done, it will surely take you to places and feelings never imagined.

The first time I met this instrument I had a feeling that somehow it was close to the guitar, but I could not pinpoint exactly how. As I learned more about Chinese music and how to play Qin, it came to me that it was just like a fretless guitar played flat on the lap. For traditional Guqin players this might sound like an abomination, but I like this approach as a way to bring more music lovers closer to the Qin and its music.

Coming from this point of view, once we place our fretless guitar on our lap, all we are missing is one string—since the Qin has seven—and to get closer to its sound range. For the latter all we need to do is to change our tuning. For the pieces in this book we will use a couple of easy tunings: D–F♯–B–D–F♯–B, and D–F–A–D–F–A. These are quite low, although not as low as Qin tunings. Still, they will work for the music and help to evoke its wonderful sounds.

If we speak about playing techniques, we will find how most right-hand guitar techniques are the same when we play this type of music. The main difference is on the left hand. But do not panic; it is not so different. First, let's see how the left-hand thumb works. Since we are playing the guitar in the lap position, our thumb is now free to press on the strings and produce different notes. In a way it is like playing piano. We will press on the strings with the left-hand fingers to produce the notes while plucking with the right hand. An advantage of this way of playing is that we can produce very subtle sound textures. By rolling our left hand fingers a little we can press the string with the skin or with the nail, producing brighter or darker sounds.

Let's try now a simple melody from the piece "The Grand Hujia." Here we are using the tuning D–F♯–B–D–F♯–B. Since it's probably the first time you are playing lap style with a fretless guitar, you might be tempted to do it in the standard position instead of on the lap. This is possible with this particular example, but as we continue you will find out how other techniques and melodies can not be performed holding the guitar in the standard way.

Example 27
Tuning (low to high) D-F♯-B-D-F♯-B

Now we have a few measures where we play melody and bass at the same time. The "p" indicator refers to the left-hand thumb. The second and third measures are played always with the thumb on the second string for continuity of sound. This excerpt comes from the piece called "Chai Tou Feng" and the guitar tuning is D–F–A–D–F–A.

Example 28
Tuning (low to high): D-F-A-D-F-A

Now that you have played this last example, try playing the melody line in the second and third measures by rolling your thumb a little in order to produce the sound with your nail (rather than skin). You will notice how the tone gets brighter. This way of playing with the nail is very useful, but keep in mind that sometimes you might have several notes connected as a glissando. If these are played on the fourth, fifth, or sixth string the nail will make a very unpleasant noise as it rubs the wound strings. In this case it is better to press with the skin to make the glissando.

GUQIN STYLE MUSIC

for Fretless Guitar

In this section we will see the Guqin style pieces, played on fretless guitar using different tunings specified in every piece.

THE GRAND HUJIA

Cai Wenji from the Han dynasty was captured during a war while out of the Great Wall. When she was finally able to return home, it was too late to see her family again; they were all gone. With the grief in her heart she composed a poem called "The Grand Hujia." This is an excerpt from the traditional Chinese music composition based on the poem.

Reading the story of the poem will help you to realize the weight in Cai Wenji's sorrow. This weight is key in the music pulse if you want to perform it correctly. A reverential attitude is often used when performing "The Grand Hujia." Exaggerating your physical movements will also help give the feel needed. I can't emphasize enough the importance of listening repeatedly to the recording and paying attention to the video explanations. The guitar tuning is D–F♯–B–D–F♯–B.

THE GRAND HUJIA

Traditional Chinese
Fretless guitar arrangement by Fernando Pérez

Tuning (low to high): D-F♯-B-D-F♯-B

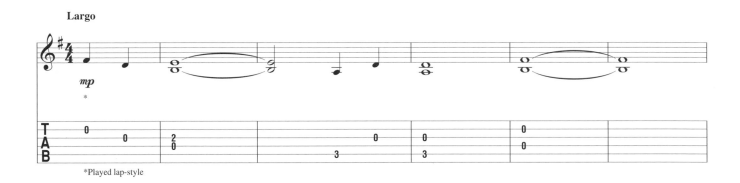

*Played lap-style

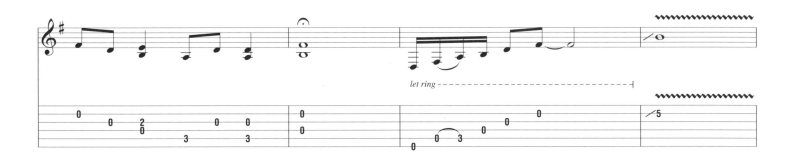

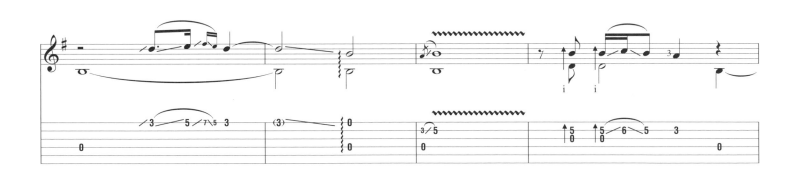

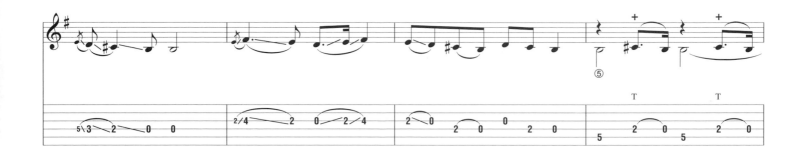

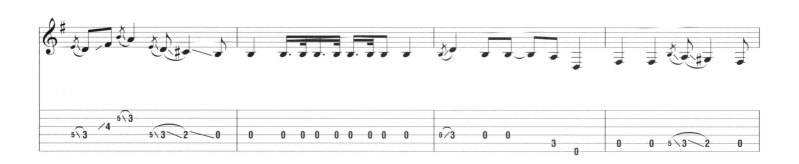

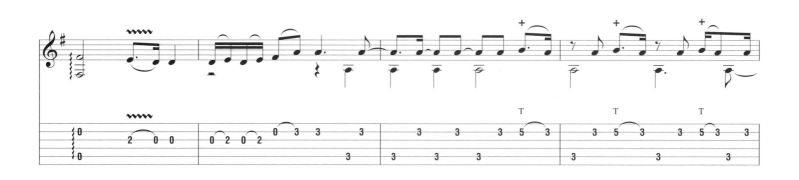

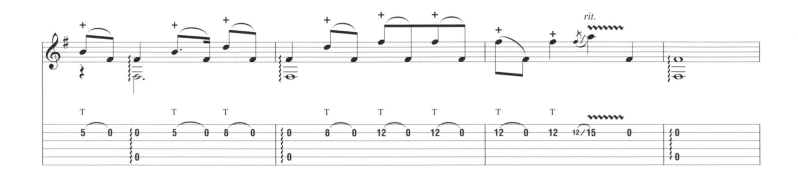

A tempo

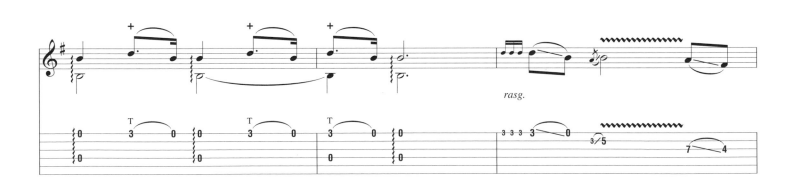

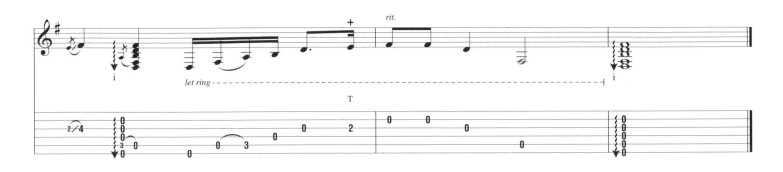

CHAI TOU FENG

Lu You was in love with Tan Wan, and when they finally were able to be together their families found reasons for them to not live happily ever after. Life continued for them afterwards, but not without much grief and longing for each other. One good day Tan Wan was strolling in the garden of Shen Yuan when her heart leaped out her chest as she saw the words from her eternal love Lu You written along the path. With tears in her eyes she wrote an answer. Unfortunatelly, that was as close as they would ever get again.

"Chai Tou Feng" is a music composition created to accompany the singing of Lu You's poem and credited to Wang Di. The piece is part of the Guqin repertoire. For this particular arrangement the most suitable guitar tuning is D–F–A–D–F–A.

CHAI TOU FENG

Music by Wang Di
Fretless guitar arrangement by Fernando Pérez

Tuning (low to high): D-F-A-D-F-A

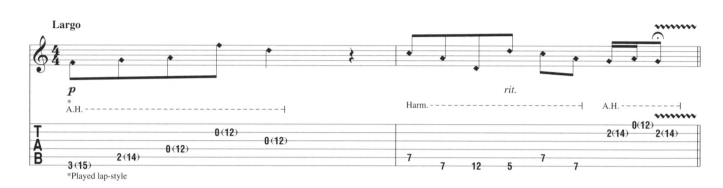

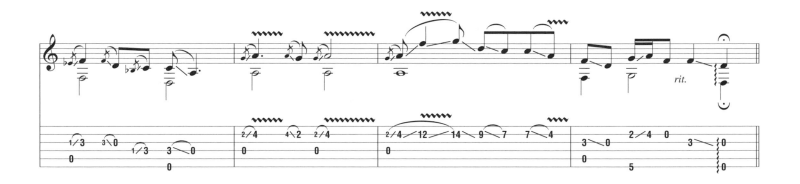

Rubato

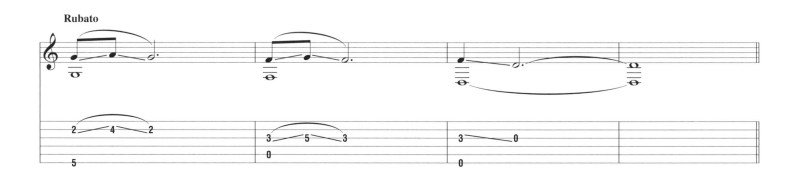

A tempo

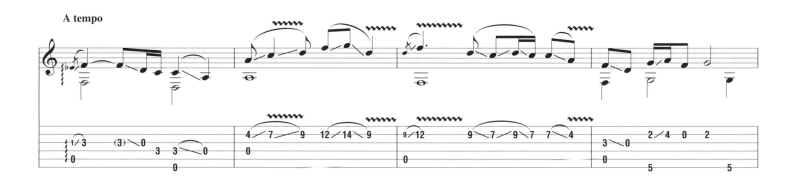

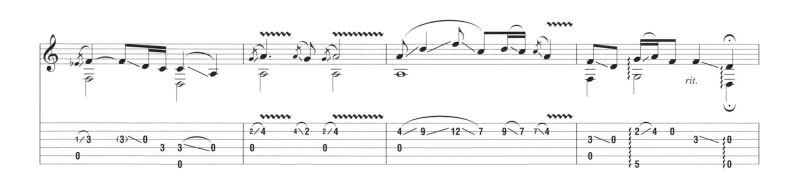

A tempo

Rubato

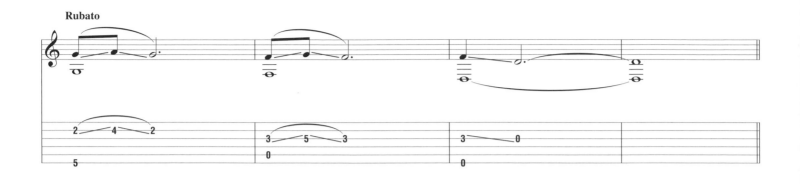

A tempo

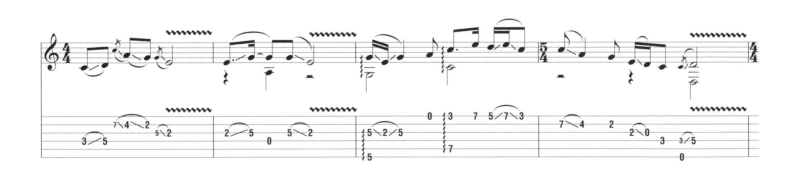

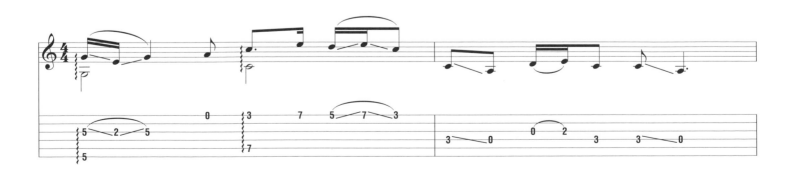

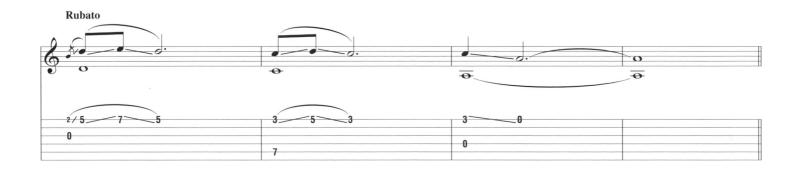

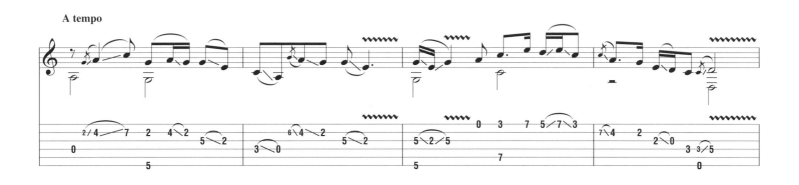

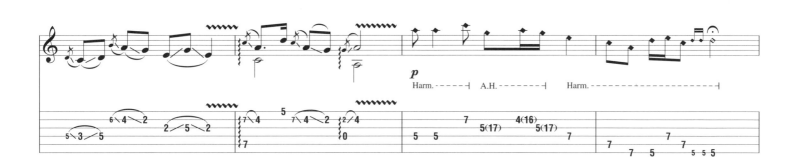

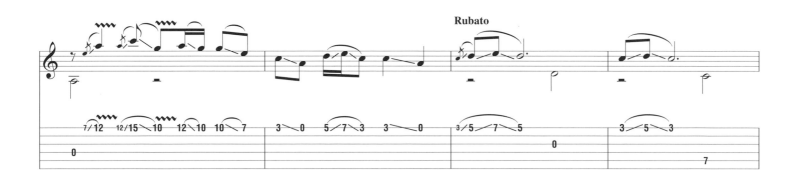

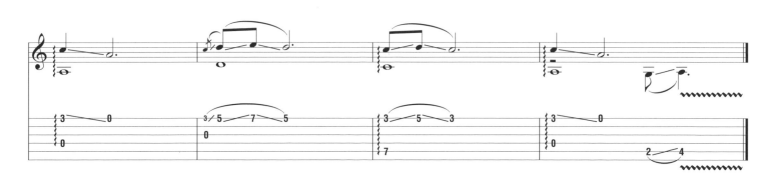

ABOUT THE AUTHOR

Born in the town of Ejea de los Caballeros, Zaragoza, Spain, Fernando's musical studies began at the age of seven. His first contact with classical music was in the conservatory of Spain. Later came numerous private instructors and music centers such as L'Aula de Musica in Barcelona, Escuela de Musica Creativa in Madrid, Musicians Institute in Hollywood, California, Maharaja Sawai Mansingh Sangeet Mahavidyalaya in Jaipur, India, Arabic Conservatoire de Musique d'Alexandrie, Egypt, Shanghai Music Conservatory in China, and Labyrinth Music Center in Greece. In these centers he studied traditional, classical and modern-contemporary music styles.

But his interest has taken him to learn more directly from artists and their cultures, traveling around the world to experience the spirit of different musical styles. He has performed with artists from such exotic places as Hawaii, West Africa, Japan, South, Central, and North America, Spain, France, Greece, Ireland, India, China, Turkey, Egypt, and more.

The guitar has always been his passion, and he explores it in many forms: Spanish classical guitar, Dobro/resophonic guitars, African guitar, Hawaiian ki Ho'alu (Slack Key) and Kika Kila (Steel Guitar), the "slide" style of Mississippi, Flamenco, the curious way of playing guitar in the Hindustani music of India, fretless Turkish and Arabic guitar, and the recently discovered Pipa and Guqin styles presented in this book.

He also explores new horizons in his arrangements and compositions based on instruments from many cultures, e.g. the Japanese Koto, Chinese Pipa and Guqin, and the African Ngoni and Kora.

His numerous performances in prestigious venues all around the world have turned Fernando Pérez into one of the leading artists dedicated to the guitar world specializing in music from different cultures. He has several published works available representing the music of the major cultures in our planet performed on guitar.

He often imparts master classes and workshops in different guitar festivals and music centers around the world, as well as collaborating in musical researches dealing with the subjects he knows best: guitar, music, and cultures.

Thanks to: Shanghai Music Conservatory, especially to Mr. Shi and Miss Guo Mei of the Traditional Chinese music department in Shanghai; Liu Fang and Risheng Wang; Jody and Kimo Huybrechts.